WOMEN AND
THE **FAMILY**

BY CAROL KIM

ReferencePoint
Press®

San Diego, CA

© 2019 ReferencePoint Press, Inc.
Printed in the United States

For more information, contact:
ReferencePoint Press, Inc.
PO Box 27779
San Diego, CA 92198
www.ReferencePointPress.com

LIBRARY OF CONGRESS CATALOGING-IN-PUBLICATION DATA

Name: Kim, Carol, 1963– author.
Title: Women and the Family/by Carol Kim.
Description: San Diego, CA: ReferencePoint Press, Inc., [2019] | Series: Women and Society
| Audience: Grade 9 to 12 | Includes bibliographical references and index.
ISBN: 978-1-68282-551-8 (hardback)
ISBN: 978-1-68282-552-5 (ebook)
The complete Library of Congress record is available at www.loc.gov.

CONTENTS

IMPORTANT EVENTS IN
WOMEN'S HISTORY

1964
The US Congress passes Title VII of the Civil Rights Act of 1964, prohibiting employment discrimination based on sex.

1920
The Nineteenth Amendment to the US Constitution gives women the right to vote.

1938
The Fair Labor Standards Act establishes a minimum wage in the United States that is the same for everyone regardless of gender.

1839
Mississippi becomes the first state to grant women the right to own property in their own names.

1840	1880	1920	1960	1970

1883
In *Pace v. Alabama*, the US Supreme Court upholds a ban on interracial marriage.

1960
The US Food and Drug Administration approves the first birth control pill.

1963
Betty Friedan's *The Feminine Mystique*, a groundbreaking book about the lives of unhappy housewives, is published.

1963
The US Congress passes the Equal Pay Act in an attempt to close the gender pay gap.

1967
In *Loving v. Virginia*, the US Supreme Court legalizes interracial marriage.

1972
Title IX is passed by the US Congress as part of the Education Amendments of 1972 to ban gender discrimination in federally funded education programs.

1993
The US Congress passes the Family and Medical Leave Act, guaranteeing twelve weeks of unpaid leave to qualifying employees for medical and family reasons.

2009
The US Congress passes the Lily Ledbetter Fair Pay Act to help prevent pay discrimination.

1975   **1985**   **1995**   **2005**   **2015**

1996
The Defense of Marriage Act is passed by the US Congress to define marriage as the union of one man and one woman.

2015
In *Obergefell v. Hodges*, the US Supreme Court legalizes same-sex marriage.

1973
In *Roe v. Wade*, the US Supreme Court legalizes abortion.

1972
The US Supreme Court legalizes birth control for all Americans.

1978
The US Congress passes the Pregnancy Discrimination Act to ban employment discrimination against pregnant women.

THE EVOLUTION OF WOMEN AND THE FAMILY

Fourteen years after 2004's *The Incredibles*, its sequel, *Incredibles 2*, picks up right where the first movie left off. But in terms of depicting women's and men's roles within the family, the 2018 sequel shows a whole new era. This time, it's mom Helen Parr, also known as Elastigirl, who has to step up and fight crime as part of a plan to help restore the reputation of superheroes. While mom is off saving the world, dad Bob Parr (Mr. Incredible) stays home to take care of the kids: teenager Violet, pre-teen Dash, and baby Jack-Jack.

While Bob struggles in the beginning, he is determined to make it work for the sake of the whole family. "I have to succeed so she can succeed . . . so *we* can succeed," Bob says.[1] This is a notable moment in the movie because it delivers an important message about how families can thrive. By providing mutual support and respect for each other, in whatever role each family member plays, everybody benefits. Elastigirl emphasizes this point when she tells Bob, "I couldn't do this if you hadn't taken over so well."[2]

In *Incredibles 2*, released in 2018, the family's mother, Elastigirl, works to save the world while her husband, Mr. Incredible, stays home to take care of the kids. This reflects the real-life trends of more women striving to balance their careers with their family lives.

A woman's relationship to her family has become increasingly complex over the past 150 years. While women don't actually have superhuman powers like Elastigirl, sometimes it can look and feel that way. Today, women are business executives and homemakers, political leaders and nurturers, professionals and volunteers, entrepreneurs and family schedulers—all at the same time.

Women have always had a prominent role in the family structure. Women are the bearers of children, and they are often the children's primary caregivers. Between mothers and fathers, mothers have traditionally carried a larger piece of the household tasks. But today, more fathers are being just like Bob Parr and embracing the role of stay-at-home dad. The Pew Research Center estimated about 2 million fathers in the United States were not working outside the home in 2012. This was out of an estimated 24.6 million fathers living in married-couple families with children younger than age eighteen.

However, while mothers and the family structure are inseparable, they are often at odds with one another. Women's quest for their own self-fulfillment over the last 150 years has often put them in direct conflict with their efforts to also be the primary caregivers in their families. Until the twentieth century, American women had little independence and very few options for how they could live their lives. Laws and customs forced women into inferior positions, subservient to and dependent on men. Author and *New York Times* columnist Gail Collins described how women were treated in the 1960s: "Everything from America's legal system to its television programs reinforced the perception that women were, in almost every way, the weaker sex."[3] Much of a woman's identity was based on her relationships to others, first as a daughter, later as a wife, and finally as a mother.

> "Everything from America's legal system to its television programs reinforced the perception that women were, in almost every way, the weaker sex."[3]
> – Gail Collins, author and New York Times *columnist*

A CHANGING ROLE

But women were not happy being confined to only one life path. Women increasingly sought to redefine their role in the family and in society. As the women's rights movement pushed for more opportunities and equal treatment for women, more women began to find fulfillment beyond their roles as homemakers. By the early twenty-first century, women made up almost one-half of the workforce, had more four-year college degrees than men, and were the sole or primary breadwinners in 40 percent of households with children younger than eighteen. The number of businesses started by women grew by 114 percent between 1997 and 2017. At the same time, a large majority of women were also having children. In 2016, 86 percent of women had given birth to at least one child by age forty-four.

In other words, women are continuing to move full tilt into both work and family. This has forced women to confront the question of how to best reconcile these two arenas—and the answer is far from clear. "We thought . . . that we could just glide into the new era of equality, with babies, board seats, and husbands in tow. We were wrong," wrote Debora Spar, former president of Barnard College.[4] As women began pursuing careers and starting families, they found that it was more complicated than they expected.

Women are also no longer adopting the traditional family structure for raising their children. Only about half of families are structured as a traditional nuclear family, which is a married couple with children. The other half of households include single-parent, multigenerational, blended (divorced parents finding new partners), and same-sex families. "The typical American family . . . has become as multilayered and full of surprises as a holiday turducken," Natalie Angier wrote for the *New York Times*.[5]

This means the world is being forced to develop a new mindset when it comes to beliefs about what it means to be a family and what it means to be a mother within that family. Sometimes the adjustment has been controversial and a source of conflict. It has forced many women to enter into uncharted territory as they seek ways to reconcile the role of women as mothers and as members of society beyond the walls of the family. Like Helen Parr's mission in *Incredibles 2*, this journey for women has been filled with episodes of extreme frustration and despair as well as triumph and exhilaration. And the journey is not over yet.

CHAPTER ONE
WHAT IS THE HISTORY BEHIND WOMEN AND THE FAMILY?

When Honey Maid, a graham cracker brand, launched its 2014 advertising campaign called This Is Wholesome, it sought to depict families of the current era in its TV commercials and other ads. One video clip from the ad campaign shows two dads taking care of their baby daughter. In another scene, a single father helps his son get dressed. A final scene shows an African American woman and her white husband together with their biracial children.

These ads were quite a departure from the era of *Ozzie and Harriet* and *Leave It to Beaver*, two popular TV shows from the 1950s that each featured a stereotypical white, middle-class family with a breadwinner father, homemaker mother, and two kids. In fact, the stereotypical American family model of the 1950s was a short-lived phenomenon. For much of history before and after this time period, families looked very different from this model. The traditional nuclear family model evolved over time, reaching its pinnacle in the 1950s, followed by a slow but steady decline.

Housewives in the 1950s were traditionally considered homemakers and were responsible for shopping, cleaning, cooking, caring for children, and other household tasks. This role was part of the stereotypical image of the nuclear family.

THE HISTORY OF MARRIAGE

Many people know the classic children's nursery rhyme, "First comes love, then comes marriage," so it may come as a surprise that for much of history, marriage was rarely based on love. Rather, in many parts of the world, from ancient times to the American Revolution, marriage was a way to preserve the economic and political status of families. This was especially true for families with large amounts of property or elite political status. For parents to allow their children to marry on the basis of such a whimsical and unstable notion as love would put the family's status and long-term future at risk. But even among lower-class families, marriage was largely based on economic and political factors. Because

11

farms and businesses could rarely be run by a single person, marriage was a way to form a partnership to support the family business. "Most women and children . . . shared the tasks of breadwinner with men. It was not unusual for wives to 'bring home the bacon'—or at least raise and slaughter the pig," historian Stephanie Coontz says.[6] Tasks were generally divided along gender lines, with men working in the fields and women focusing on household tasks. Colonial families were large, and women gave birth to an average of seven to ten children. Having many children was necessary because children often died, largely due to the absence of advanced medicine.

A woman's role in the family was primarily to serve her husband, and in that role she was completely dependent on him for survival. "Woman was the 'weaker vessel,' the 'softer' sex, inferior in reason to man, created to serve a husband and nurture children," wrote Marilyn Yalom in *A History of the Wife*.[7] In fact, a woman's legal existence disappeared upon marriage. A wife was incorporated into her husband's citizenship under a legal doctrine in both Great Britain and the United States called coverture. After marriage, a woman could not own property (even property she owned before her marriage), enter into contracts, or sue or be sued in her own name.

THE SHIFT TO LOVE

The Age of Enlightenment during the eighteenth century introduced what was then the radical notion of living for the pursuit of happiness. In keeping with this notion, love and affection began to be seen as the primary basis for marriage. Couples came together for affection, friendship, respect, and shared interests. The Victorian period in America saw a move toward making marriage the essential goal and experience of people's lives.

But even as love raised couples' satisfaction with marriage as a meaningful relationship, it also decreased the stability of marriage as an institution. As Coontz explained: "If marriage was about love and lifelong intimacy, why would people marry at all if they couldn't find true love?"[8] Further, once people got married, why would they continue to stay together if their love and affection disappeared?

The early twentieth century saw a large increase in young women and men socializing on their own terms, without the close supervision of their parents. The 1920s was the era of the Roaring Twenties

> "If marriage was about love and lifelong intimacy, why would people marry at all if they couldn't find true love?"[8]
> – Stephanie Coontz, historian

and the Jazz Age, where women cast aside conservative conventions that prescribed how they should dress and behave. Women dressed in new fashions and fads, giving rise to the flapper style of shorter skirts and dresses with beads and fringe. Single women enjoyed a new level of independence. Women and men continued to marry, however, as often as ever.

The end of the Jazz Age came suddenly with the 1929 stock market crash and eventual economic collapse in the United States and around the world. The Great Depression tested the stability of families. With high levels of unemployment and wages falling, Americans were forced to delay marriage and having children. While divorce rates fell, it was largely because divorce was too expensive for many couples. However, the number of people who abandoned their spouses increased. Despite the job shortages, more women actually entered the workforce during this time to make extra money for their families. Even young children had to work to help keep families afloat.

Young adults in the 1920s had more independence than in the past. This included more socializing without their parents and new fashion options, such as this woman's outfit.

The Depression ended largely because of the start of World War II (1939–1945). Men and women rushed to get married in record numbers— but then as families suffered because of the war, the divorce rate rose. Also during World War II, married women poured into the workforce. The number of women in the workforce increased by almost 60 percent between 1940 and 1945. Many women started working in jobs that had previously only allowed male workers. This included jobs as mechanics, welders, and carpenters. These women were also paid wages more in line with men's wages. Most African American women had already been working before the war, but their jobs were largely limited to menial and low-paying housework. With the labor shortage, black women were able to get higher-paid manufacturing jobs or white-collar jobs.

At the end of the war, however, women were pushed out of their jobs to make way for the returning veterans. Many returned home to start a family, but others protested losing their jobs, and some continued to work out of financial necessity. The women who preferred life as a wage earner found that society could be highly critical of them. An article in *The Atlantic* magazine lamented, "What ails these women who consciously or unconsciously reject their children?"[9]

Following the stresses of the Depression era and the war, many women and men eagerly jumped into marrying and starting families. The average age of women marrying dropped to twenty, divorce rates stabilized, and the number of births almost doubled. The GI Bill, a law created to financially assist veterans when they returned home from war, was signed into law in 1944. The bill helped veterans pay for college, find good-paying jobs, and purchase homes in the suburbs. However, many black veterans did not receive the same benefits that white veterans did. Many black veterans were refused access to financial loans and job placement assistance programs, and many were directed to vocational schools rather than four-year colleges. Still, the GI Bill overall helped almost 9 million veterans.

This brought America into the era of the 1950s idyllic family life. Fathers took the role of breadwinner while mothers stayed home to care for the children and household. As families spent quality time together, *Leave It to Beaver* and *Ozzie and Harriet* appeared on television screens to reinforce the stereotype of the white, married, suburban family. But these images were misleading, especially for non-white families. One African American woman remembers watching these TV shows as a young girl and thinking, "Why didn't we live in a house with a back yard and a front yard instead of an old apartment?"[10] A significant portion of families did not fit the TV stereotype. "Only 60 percent of children born during that decade spent their childhoods in a male-breadwinner,

Not all families of the 1950s had the idealized breadwinner father, homemaker mother, and two kids in a suburban house. In reality, most families did not fit into that stereotype, including this family with several children living in an apartment.

female-homemaker household," explained Steven Mintz, a historian at the University of Texas at Austin.[11]

By the 1970s, women began waiting longer to get married. As women gained experience from work and school, they also gained self-confidence and began to seek fulfillment beyond marriage. As their horizons began to open up, women became increasingly frustrated by the limits placed on their progress. The women's rights movement blossomed and boosted women's entry into the workforce and higher education. Birth control became widely available to women for the first time with the release of the birth control pill in 1960. In 1973, the Supreme Court guaranteed a woman's right to an abortion in the landmark case *Roe v. Wade.*

Another important force changing American families was the increase in working women. The number of working women climbed steeply after 1960. This afforded women greater independence, including financial independence. Women no longer needed to get married or stay married if a marriage was unsatisfactory.

Also during this time period, the Supreme Court struck down laws preventing interracial marriage, further transforming the image of an American family. The court's decision in *Loving v. Virginia* legalized interracial marriage in 1967.

The early twenty-first century saw major changes in the treatment of gay and lesbian families. Same-sex couples began to be granted the same kind of legal protections that had previously been given to only heterosexual married couples. In 2015, a US Supreme Court ruling legalized gay marriage across the country.

In 1960, 70 percent of American households were made up of a working father, a stay-at-home mother, and two or more kids. By 2010, the figure had dropped to 45 percent of all households. By 2016, it was only about a quarter of families. More and more families were looking like those shown in the Honey Maid ads.

WOMEN'S ROLE IN THE FAMILY

During the nineteenth century, when America was moving further away from an agricultural society and toward an industrial one, more men left home for jobs in the city. Women stayed home to care for the children and manage the household. These distinct gender roles came to be referred to as "the doctrine of separate spheres."[12]

In this theory, the separate duties of husbands and wives were supposed to carry equal worth. The arrangement was seen as a partnership between a husband and wife, with each contributing to the welfare of the family. But the growing industrial economy led to continued inequality between husbands and wives. Because men were the wage earners and still controlled the finances of the family, wives continued to be dependent on their husbands. The notion that a woman's role was to stay at home and take care of all the household affairs, including taking care of the children, persisted for decades. Despite their increased participation in the workforce during World War II, women were encouraged to leave their jobs when the war ended.

Following the war, as families entered the era of the traditional marriage, more families than ever before enjoyed a decent standard of living on only one income (usually the father's income). But for many women who were full-time homemakers, the monotony, drudgery, and isolation of their lives was deeply unsatisfying. By the 1960s, women began to feel limited in their role as housewives. When Betty Friedan's book *The Feminine Mystique* was published in 1963, it hit a nerve among these women. Friedan gave voice to the guilt and yearning of women who felt unfulfilled by their roles as wives and mothers. Friedan wrote: "She was afraid to ask even of herself the silent question—'Is this all?'"[13]

Women from working-class families during this era were generally more accepting of the traditional roles of husbands and wives. For the most part, a man did not want his wife working outside the home because it made it appear that he couldn't adequately provide for his family. In addition, most working-class men believed they shouldn't have to help with the housekeeping once they came home from work. In four-fifths of families, the cooking, cleaning, and laundry were all the responsibility of the wives.

Between 1965 and 2010, married women reduced their time spent on housework in half, while married men doubled theirs. Women had been spending seven times as many hours on housework as their husbands, but by 2010 this had changed, and women were spending twice as much time as men on housework. While fewer women worked in 1965, research

In 1963, *The Feminine Mystique* publicly highlighted the boredom and isolation that many housewives were feeling at the time. Through the 1960s, more and more women began to leave their traditional homemaker roles to join the workforce.

shows they actually spent less time on childcare than women in 2010, instead spending more time on housework and leisure. Husbands overall also increased their time with the kids between 1965 and 2010. Still, the amount of time women spend on childcare is almost double that of men.

MOTHERHOOD

The roots of women's larger role in childcare may have started during the Victorian era, from the mid- to late-1800s. During this period, society believed a wife achieved her greatest purpose in life when she became

WOMEN OF THE WESTWARD EXPANSION

During the 1800s, middle- and upper-class white women were cloaked with the virtues of religiousness, purity, submissiveness, and domesticity. But these traits did little to serve women who moved to the American west in the mid-1800s. These women mined, drove wagons, managed farms and ranches, and opened stores and schools, all alongside their husbands. Luzena Wilson, who went with her husband to California during the Gold Rush, wrote: "Yes, we worked; we did things that [people] would now look at aghast, and say it was impossible for a woman to do." Not only did these women work—they faced dangers and hardships such as accidents, disease, prairie fires, floods, and sudden disaster. But they also gained more freedoms, such as the right to own land. In contrast, the migration's effect on Native American women already living in the west was catastrophic. White people destroyed food sources and brought disease. Native women faced extreme poverty and the loss of their way of life. But both groups of women had one shared experience. They demonstrated that women were strong and resourceful.

Quoted in JoAnn Levy, They Saw the Elephant: Women in the California Gold Rush. *Norman, Oklahoma: University of Oklahoma Press, 1992, p. 98.*

a mother. At the same time, parents' view of children and childhood began to change. Previously, children were seen as miniature adults who had a natural tendency to be wicked and depraved. Parents believed children needed to be controlled through harsh discipline and hard work. Children were often sent away to live and work in the homes of others starting at age ten or eleven. But during the Victorian era, parents began to see children as innocent and precious. Childhood was viewed as a special time, and parents, especially mothers, cherished and nurtured their children. Children began to be the central focus of the family, perhaps even the main reason for a family's existence.

As America entered the twentieth century, women had fewer and fewer children. White women had an average of 3.6 children in 1900. That number fell to 2.3 children by 1940. But after World War II, everything changed. The instability of the Depression and war years caused men and women to seek security and comfort in families. They flocked to marriage and had children—a lot of children. The number of babies born jumped

20 percent between 1945 and 1946. A steady increase in births continued for almost two decades. This was the baby boom era, which lasted from 1946 to 1964.

Following the baby boom, birth rates began a steady decline that has continued into the twenty-first century. From 1900 to 2010, the birth rate fell about 60 percent. In 1900, there were thirty-two births per 1,000 people in the United States. By 2010, the rate had dropped to thirteen births per 1,000 people.

Children who grew up in the 1970s and 1980s describe lives as so-called "latchkey kids" (kids left on their own during the after-school hours before a parent returned home from work). They were less involved in scheduled after-school activities such as sports or summer camps compared with many children today. Parents generally took a relaxed approach to raising these kids. Mother Shannon Bradley-Colleary described playing outside as a child: "A lot of my favorite memories were playing 'war' . . . until well after dark, with no one even calling to see where I was."[14]

By the end of the twentieth century, a more child-centered parenting approach became popular. As many women had fewer children later in life and had busier schedules as they worked outside the home, they also began to focus more intensely on how they raised their children. Lisen Stromberg, author of *Work Pause Thrive*, describes this parenting approach: "The truth is mothering hasn't just become who we are; it has become what we do—our new full-time job."[15]

By the early 2000s, women had started embracing the ideal of a stereotypical "Uber Mommy"—the perfect mother who did it all. Mothers believed they needed to feed

"The truth is mothering hasn't just become who we are; it has become what we do—our new full-time job."[15]
– *Lisen Stromberg, author of Work Pause Thrive*

their children the best food (breastmilk for babies, organic food for the rest), expose them to stimuli to build their IQs, enroll them in numerous after-school activities, and protect them from any possible harm. By the next decade, new terms to describe modern parenting began to sprout. Instead of raising latchkey kids, now parents engaged in helicopter parenting—hovering and overfocusing on their children. Many credit the change to increased societal pressure on mothers to be perfect parents. Another factor could be parents trying to be different from their own less-protective parents.

WORKING WOMEN

One of the most significant developments affecting women's relationships to their families is their involvement in the workforce. Women have always worked, but it was not always for pay outside the home. In early colonial America, every member of the family pitched in to keep the family business or farm running. While women of the colonial period mostly worked in their homes for no pay, they were producing significant amounts of goods and services. Most African American women were forced into this work as unpaid slaves.

By the late nineteenth century, women gradually began to leave the home and work in America's growing number of factories. Because wages for women were low, there were still economic benefits for them to marry. However, single women were increasingly able to earn a living, causing them to reconsider whether marriage was still a valuable option. This was especially true for educated women.

By the mid-1800s, more than 1 million workers could be found in manufacturing. About a quarter of these workers were women, the highest proportion at any time in the century. But most women left their jobs when they married. Society frowned upon wives working outside the home.

Through the 1970s, 1980s, and 1990s, more and more women began getting jobs outside of their homes, learning to balance motherhood and their careers. By the twenty-first century, women made up approximately half of the workforce in the United States.

For working-class families, it was usually not possible to live only on the earnings of the father. Because they no longer worked in outside jobs, married women sought different ways to make money while staying at home. Many provided products or services from home, including creating embroideries, making artificial flowers, making clothes, or doing laundry. Another option for families was to have renters live in their homes.

More women joined the workforce in the early 1900s, with many women taking secretarial jobs as the number of office jobs in the United States increased. African American women living in the rural South worked mostly in low-paid service or farm labor jobs. Women continued to work during World War II when they were encouraged to take the jobs that soldiers left behind. Progress somewhat stalled when the war ended and many women were pushed out of the workforce by the men who returned home. Yet, despite the remaining barriers to joining the workforce, women continued to do so. In 1950, 29 percent of workers were women. That figure rose to 40 percent by 1975. More women continued to work after getting married, or they left the workforce but returned when their children began to go to school. These women were not just putting in part-time hours, either. By 1975, more than 70 percent of women who worked had full-time jobs.

By 2016, women made up close to half of the workforce in America, at 46.8 percent. Of all women, 56.8 percent were working. Seventy percent of all mothers with children younger than eighteen were in the workforce, and many had become the primary or sole breadwinners for their families. Women held this breadwinner position in 40 percent of households with children, compared with only 11 percent in 1960. African American mothers are the breadwinners in 80 percent of their households. Three-quarters of them are also the sole family income earner.

Historically, women have been paid less than men, even for the same work. This difference, called the *wage gap,* has continued into the present day, although the gap has narrowed over time. While the wage gap has been measured between all men and women, the gap between the wages of white men and Hispanic, black, and Asian women is even higher.

While many married women work out of financial necessity, they are also doing it because of the personal satisfaction they get from their jobs.

"Women who work, including mothers, are consistently found to be healthier, less depressed, and less frustrated than women who do not," historian Coontz says.[16] Today, many women have said they get more respect, both from their husbands and from society, when they have a job. By bringing in an income, women also tend to have more decision-making power in their marriages than wives who don't work. Coontz's research also shows that the more a woman contributed to the family's joint income, the more her husband helped with the housework and childcare.

> "Women who work, including mothers, are consistently found to be healthier, less depressed, and less frustrated than women who do not."[16]
> – Stephanie Coontz, historian

The struggle of women to raise their status equal to men in both the family and the workplace has made great progress during the course of American history. As women continue expanding their role in the world outside of their families, they are facing new challenges.

CHAPTER TWO

WHAT CHALLENGES DO MODERN FAMILIES FACE?

Over the last 200 years, the relationship between women and the family has undergone some radical changes. By rejecting society's premise that women are subordinate to men and in need of protection, women have forced open doors for themselves beyond the family. In doing do, women have also changed some of the fundamental aspects of the family structure and its purpose. As a result, marriage, parenting, and the working world have also had to adjust. While most women agree that they are better off than in the past, new challenges have emerged. As women, men, and society as a whole grapple with these challenges, the family will continue to be reshaped and evolve. Yet, on the other hand, the basic premise of family endures. Even as the family structure is modified and reconstructed, it continues to serve as a source of financial and emotional support to its members and plays a vital role in society.

THE STATE OF MARRIAGE

People have been predicting the demise of marriage for decades. In 1928, John Watson, a famous child psychiatrist, predicted that marriage

Research shows that people are waiting longer to get married, and many couples are choosing to live together and start their families without getting married. This contributes to an overall decline in the number of marriages in the United States.

would be dead by 1977. Then, in 1977, Amitai Etzioni, a noted sociologist, made the pronouncement that "by mid-1990 not one American family will be left."[17] While these dire predictions obviously did not come to pass, concerns about the future of marriage continue. As recently as 2010, a poll by the Pew Research Center found that 50 percent of younger Americans and 40 percent of all Americans believe that "marriage is becoming obsolete."[18]

The truth is, Americans' participation in the institution of marriage has been falling steadily since the end of the baby boom years in the mid-1960s. Today, one-half of all American adults are married, and this percentage has remained steady in recent years. However, there has been a 9 percent decline in marriage over the last twenty-five years, and marriages are significantly less common than in 1960, when 72 percent of adults were married.

One reason for the decline in marriage is the fact that men and women are waiting longer to get married. In 1960, the average age of men marrying for the first time was 22.8, and for women it was 20.3. By 2016, the average ages of men and women entering their first marriages were 29.5 and 27.4, respectively.

Waiting longer to get married is only part of the reason for the decline in marriages overall. A greater share of Americans than ever before have never married, and the numbers have been rising over the last few decades. Men and women are choosing different arrangements, including living with a partner without marriage (also called cohabitating) and having children outside of marriage.

WHAT DO FAMILIES LOOK LIKE TODAY?

With fewer couples getting married and divorce still ending almost one-half of all marriages, families are looking quite a bit different from the 1950s traditional family. Instead, many children are living in blended families. These families include people who have remarried after divorce, bringing their children with them to a new family and having additional children with a new spouse. The US Census Bureau reported 7.5 percent of children lived with at least one stepparent in 2010. Almost half of people ages eighteen to twenty-nine, and 23 percent of those ages fifty to sixty-four, have a stepsibling. Blended families also include single-parent families, families with adopted children, grandparents raising their grandchildren, couples with adopted children, and foster families.

CHANGES IN FAMILY LIVING ARRANGEMENTS FOR
CHILDREN IN THE UNITED STATES

	1960	1980	2014
Two parents in first marriage	73%	61%	46%
Two parents in remarriage	14%	16%	15%
Cohabitating parents	–	–	7%
Single parent	9%	19%	26%
No parent	4%	4%	5%

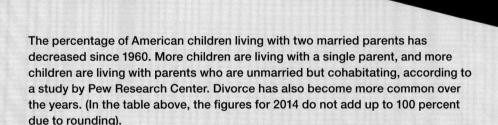

The percentage of American children living with two married parents has decreased since 1960. More children are living with a single parent, and more children are living with parents who are unmarried but cohabitating, according to a study by Pew Research Center. Divorce has also become more common over the years. (In the table above, the figures for 2014 do not add up to 100 percent due to rounding).

"The American Family Today," Pew Research Center, *December 17, 2015.*
www.pewsocialtrends.org.

The rise in single-parent families has been dramatic. In 1960, 87 percent of children were being raised by two married parents, compared with 9 percent being raised by single parents. In 2009, only 64.7 percent of children were living in families with two married parents, while 27.3 percent were in single-parent families.

The number of births to unmarried mothers peaked in 2008, with 51.8 births per 1,000 women between ages fifteen and forty-four. Since then, that number dropped to 44.8 births in 2013, a decline of 14 percent. Between 2007 and 2012, births to unmarried teens dropped the most, declining by 30 percent. The declines were sharpest for black and Hispanic women (11 percent and 28 percent decreases, respectively). Researchers examined possible reasons for this decrease. One reason is that birth rates fell when the economy suffered, particularly during the recession from 2007 to 2009. Other factors contributing to the continued decline include more effective birth control and pregnancy prevention programs aimed at teens.

Unmarried women having children are not necessarily parenting alone. In 2010, more than half (58 percent) of unmarried mothers were cohabiting. This is an increase from 2002, when 41 percent of unmarried mothers were living with a partner. One of the greatest challenges to single parenthood is being limited to one income and one caregiver. Single-parent families are more likely to be living in poverty, especially when the household is headed by the mother. Children in these families have been shown to drop out of school at higher rates and to be more likely to abuse drugs and alcohol. Cohabiting families could provide more social and financial support than households in which women are raising their children alone.

One group of women deliberately deciding to have children on their own may be able to overcome the risks to their children caused by

BIRTH CONTROL NOW AND IN THE FUTURE

Birth control is often used by women who are planning when and how they want to have children and grow their families. It also helps women who never want to have children. Some contraceptives use hormones, such as the pill (including the morning-after pill), the patch (worn on the body), the vaginal ring (inserted into the vagina), and the shot (injected monthly). Others use a barrier method, such as condoms, diaphragms, sponges, and cervical caps, which are inserted before intercourse. Some birth control methods are long-lasting, such as the IUD (intrauterine device, inserted into the uterus for five to ten years) or implants (inserted into the arm every three years).

Innovative new methods are also being developed. One is the fertility chip, a remote-controlled implant that could last for up to sixteen years. Others include a contraceptive ring that lasts for a year, an improved female condom, and a gel that is rubbed into and absorbed by the skin.

It's usually women who take responsibility for birth control. But new options for men are being developed, too. These include various types of male pills and a male injection which blocks sperm from leaving the body.

single parenthood. These are single women older than thirty-five, mostly college educated, who were having children at a rate 48 percent higher in 2012 than in 2002. They are established in their careers and financially secure. How are these women becoming mothers? Some adopt children. Others choose to become pregnant on their own. The most common methods for this are artificial insemination (where sperm is inserted directly into the womb by a doctor), in-vitro fertilization (where the egg and sperm are combined in a laboratory dish and the resulting embryo is implanted into the womb), and with help from donor sperm banks (a facility that collects and stores sperm from donors). Many women in this group feel they shouldn't have to give up motherhood just because they're not in a relationship with a man. One woman, Jennifer Williams, a gerontologist in California, explained, "I was 40 and dating and dating and dating and just not having any luck."[19] She became pregnant after six attempts through a sperm donor and had her daughter, Maya. "It's absolutely the best thing I ever did," she said.[20]

MORE RACIAL DIVERSITY IN FAMILIES

At the end of the 1920s, forty-two US states had laws in place banning interracial marriage. These laws began to be repealed in the 1950s. But it wasn't until 1967, when the US Supreme Court ruled in *Loving v. Virginia*, that marriage between people of different races became legal across the country. Since then, interracial marriage has increased steadily from 3 percent in 1967 to 17 percent of newlyweds in 2015. Among all married Americans, 10 percent, or 11 million people, are married to a person of a different race or ethnicity.

Public acceptance of interracial marriage has grown steadily over the years. While 24 percent of American adults believed marrying between different races was good for society in 2010, that figure grew to 39 percent by 2016. As of 2017, interracial marriages in the United States were most common between one Hispanic and one white spouse, making up 42 percent of these marriages. Second-most common were marriages between Asian and white spouses (15 percent), then white and multiracial spouses (12 percent), and then black and white spouses (11 percent).

The overall increase in interracial marriage has also resulted in a steady rise in multiracial children (children of two or more races) born in the United States. The percentage has grown from 5 percent of the population in 1980 to 14 percent by 2015. According to the American Academy of Child and Adolescent Psychiatry, multiracial children face some unique challenges. Some report feeling pressure to identify with only one race. Others have experienced teasing, discrimination, or unwanted attention because of their mixed-race backgrounds. Multiracial children are also often able to be more open to and understanding of cultural diversity among others. Through their own family experiences, they learn to how to navigate various racial and cultural aspects outside their families as well.

Since interracial marriage was legalized in the United States in 1967, it has become increasingly common. More mixed-race children are being born in the United States.

TOGETHER WITHOUT MARRIAGE

Cohabitation, which is defined as living together as a sexual or romantic couple outside of marriage, has become more common over the last decade in America. In 2016, the number of adults in the United States living with someone outside of marriage was 18 million. That's an increase of 29 percent from 2007. Around 14 percent of Americans between ages twenty-five and thirty-four were cohabitating. Concerns about the rise in cohabitation stem from the disadvantages these families experience compared with families headed by married couples. Cohabitating families tend to be less stable, with couples more likely to split up, and they generally are not as strong financially.

So, why not marry? Many couples believe living together is a way to do a trial run on their relationship before taking the bigger step of marriage. Others lack confidence that a marriage will last and choose cohabitation as a living arrangement with no intention of eventually tying the knot. Research analyst Renee Stepler found that many couples wanted to avoid the emotional, legal, and financial strains of divorce.

The biggest increase in cohabitation has happened among adults older than fifty. This has increased 75 percent over the last decade, surprising many researchers. Stepler noted, "Cohabiting adults 50 and older make up one-quarter of all cohabiters today, and that's striking because cohabitation used to be a step before marriage."[21] Older adults choosing to live together without marriage are likely doing so for reasons different than their younger counterparts. They may be looking for companionship and a wider social life to avoid the feelings of isolation that can be common for this age group, especially if a person is widowed or divorced. Helping one another out financially can also benefit both parties.

CHANGING ROLES WITHIN MARRIAGE

Most of society believes it is a man's responsibility to be the primary financial provider in a family, even as women's place in the workforce has grown and their earning power has increased. In one-third of married or cohabitating couples, women contribute half or more of the earnings. According to a Pew Research Center survey, roughly 71 percent of adults believe it is very important for a man to be able to support a family to be a good spouse. Only 32 percent say the same for women.

But a study of men and women ages eighteen to thirty-two found that they would like more equal roles within the family. If the necessary support was available through affordable and high-quality childcare and

Research shows that most adults younger than thirty-two would like to equally share housework and familial tasks with their partners. But, in heterosexual relationships, women generally still take on more of these tasks, despite the fact that many of these women have jobs like their husbands.

flexible work schedules, a majority of men and women in the study said they would choose an equal division of responsibilities. But without this support, women are more likely to stay at home or reduce their work hours for the children. Sarah Thébaud, a sociologist who coauthored the study, explained to National Public Radio, "Raising children when both parents work full time at demanding jobs is very difficult."[22] The challenge often pushes women to leave work or work part time.

There are different reasons behind why it is more likely for mothers, rather than fathers, to pull back on their jobs for their families. It could be that it is just personally harder for women to prioritize their jobs over taking care of their children. One study showed that the conflict between work and family has emotional and psychological effects on women. Shira Offer of Bar-Ilan University in Israel, who led the study, found that men and women both spend about equal amounts of time thinking about their family's needs. The difference is that men are not as negatively affected by this thinking. For women, thinking about family matters caused significant negative emotional responses, including guilt and stress. Sheryl Sandberg, chief operating officer (COO) of Facebook, explained, "I feel guilty when my son says, 'Mommy, put down the BlackBerry, talk to me.' I think all women feel guilty. I don't know a lot of men who feel guilty for working full time, it's expected that they'll work full time."[23] On the other hand, more dads than moms think they don't spend enough time with the kids. The biggest obstacle to family time for men is time on the job. Still, fathers are spending more time with their children than they were fifty years ago.

> "I think all women feel guilty. I don't know a lot of men who feel guilty for working full time, it's expected that they'll work full time."[23]
> – Sheryl Sandberg, COO of Facebook

However, unlike in heterosexual relationships, research shows that same-sex couples tend to divide chores more equally or perceive the division of family labor as more equal. In couples where one partner earns more, the other is more likely to take up more of the household tasks. But even with one partner shouldering more of the childcare and other household responsibilities, gay and lesbian parents generally felt it was an equitable division. Same-sex couples tended to divide up these tasks based on personal preferences rather than gender roles.

THE MYTH OF PERFECT MOTHERS

In 2014, greeting card company American Greetings produced a video titled *World's Toughest Job*. In it, applicants for a director of operations job are given a list of requirements: no sitting, no breaks, unlimited hours, and excellent negotiation and interpersonal skills. Preferred degrees for applicants are in medicine, finance, or the culinary arts. The work must be done while maintaining a happy disposition. The pay for all this hard work? Absolutely nothing. As the applicants look on in disbelief, the interviewer reveals that billions of people do this job—moms.

While the message, of course, is a tribute to the hard work of mothers everywhere, it is also an example of how the media promotes an idealized image of mothers. This ideal mother is called upon to wear many hats. Just as the American Greetings ad portrayed mothers' need for versatility, moms are called upon to be therapists, pediatricians, caretakers, homemakers, and mind readers. Susan Douglas, coauthor of *The Mommy Myth*, dubbed this role "the new Momism."[24] She describes it as "a highly romanticized myth of the perfect mother. It's a role no woman can ever attain. Her 'to do' list includes: piping Mozart into her womb, using algebra flash cards with her 6-month-old, teaching her 3-year-old to read James Joyce, driving five hours to a soccer match, and oh, yes, being sexy and cheerful through all of this."[25]

Time magazine devoted the front-page story of an October 2017 issue to this idealized portrait of motherhood, calling it "the Goddess Myth."[26] By trying to place society's impossible standards on themselves, these mothers are experiencing higher levels of stress and depression, causing them to parent less effectively. "With my first [child], I found myself really stressed out trying to live up to it all and embarrassed when I couldn't," said Seana Norvell, a California mom.[27] Tennessee mother Kaitlyn Kambestad added, "As a new mom, it's easy to feel judged. There are so many conflicting studies, ideas and opinions. It's overwhelming."[28]

"As a new mom, it's easy to feel judged. There are so many conflicting studies, ideas and opinions. It's overwhelming."[28]
– *Kaitlyn Kambestad, Tennessee mother*

THE MOMMY WARS

The pressure that mothers place on themselves to be perfect parents is also fueled by pressure coming from other mothers. The practice of mothers criticizing other mothers has become so widespread, it was even given a label: the Mommy Wars. Also referred to as mom shaming, it usually involves judgement around the choices mothers are making regarding feeding, discipline, or whether one stays home with the kids or works outside the home at a job. Many are guilty of participating; in a poll conducted by *Parenting* magazine, 97 percent of respondents admitted to criticizing other parents. Celebrities are common targets of this criticism. Model Chrissy Teigen has been attacked for how she dresses her children, what she feeds them, and everything in between. Model Coco Rocha was criticized when she revealed she fed her daughter baby formula. A national poll conducted by the C.S. Mott Children's Hospital at the University of Michigan found four out of ten mothers had received criticism that made them feel unsure about their parenting skills. Topics most commonly targeted include discipline (70 percent), diet and nutrition (52 percent), breastfeeding or bottle-feeding (39 percent), safety (20 percent), and childcare (16 percent).

Karen Johnson, a stay-at-home mom (SAHM), has discouraged mom shaming in writing on her blog, *The 21st Century SAHM*. She confessed: "My house is never clean. Like ever. I have friends (with kids) whose houses are spotless. Are they better mothers than me? Nope. Am I a better mother than them? Nope."[29] The post went viral, getting 650,000 likes and 400,000 shares on her blogging platform, clearly striking a chord with the public. Many comments were very supportive, such as this one by Janet McEuen:

> "My house is never clean. Like ever. I have friends (with kids) whose houses are spotless. Are they better mothers than me? Nope. Am I a better mother than them? Nope."[29]
>
> *– Karen Johnson, stay-at-home mom and blogger*

"Truth in every word and I'm tickled you had the guts to put it out there. Seems to me like you're a wonderful mother."[30] Yet, despite the message behind her post, Johnson was still attacked by others. "Maybe you should clean your house instead of exercising," wrote one reader. "I think it's more important to have a clean and sanitized home for the health of your family. Do exercises while you clean."[31]

THE CHALLENGES OF CHILDCARE

One of the biggest challenges facing families today is the struggle to find affordable, good-quality childcare. The disappearance of families with one breadwinner and one full-time caregiver in the United States means that nearly 11 million children younger than age five spend time in some type of childcare every week. Only 23 percent of mothers and 3 percent of fathers are stay-at-home parents.

Parents magazine conducted a survey in December 2017, and 84 percent of respondents said that finding affordable, quality childcare is either challenging, very hard, or impossible. According to the organization Child Care Aware of America, the cost of childcare has increased twice as fast as the median income of families since 2000. Fees range from $3,900 a year in Mississippi to $15,000 a year in Massachusetts, depending on the age of the child and the type of care. With the median income for families at just over $55,000 a year and infant childcare costing an average of $10,000 a year, many families are faced with difficult choices.

This was the case for Meredith and Paul Tweed of Longwood, Florida. After the birth of their first son, they found a daycare provider who cared for children in her own home for $500 a month, which was half the cost of a daycare center nearby. When the Tweeds' second child came along, their monthly childcare bill doubled. To save money, they sold their town house and moved in with Meredith's parents for a year. Meredith changed jobs, and the couple bought a house (a fixer-upper to save money), canceled cable TV, and decided to not have any more children. Together,

Most parents in the United States struggle with the high costs of childcare. Some families plan most of their other expenses around their childcare bills.

the couple makes $72,000 a year, and childcare takes 17 percent of their income. Their monthly childcare bill is $1,100 a month, which is just $28 less than their mortgage payment. This childcare bill is twice as much as the cost of tuition and fees at Florida State University.

For low-income and single-parent families, the situation is even more difficult. The federal government provides financial assistance to low-income families through the Child Care and Development Block Grant (CCDBG). But only a small fraction of families receives these benefits because the grant has limited funding. Only 16 percent of children eligible for assistance received it in 2013.

On the other side are the childcare providers themselves. These workers play an important role—taking care of young children—and yet they only make about $23,800 a year on average. Childcare providers need money to pay for rent, utilities, food, and maintenance, along with employee salaries. Because good childcare requires low staff-to-child ratios, simply letting in more children to make more money is not feasible. There is little a facility can do to raise salaries except to raise tuition costs, and the tuitions are already too high for many families to afford. The resulting low wages paid to childcare workers make it hard to attract and retain well-qualified workers. It also makes it difficult for childcare workers, who are mostly women, to support their own families.

The challenge of childcare in the United States is widespread, and many feel it is not getting the attention it deserves. Donna Denette, executive director of Children First, a childcare center in Massachusetts, said: "Imagine if all the childcare centers closed for a week. Everything would come to a screeching halt. But you don't hear people talking about us as if we're critical to the functioning of society."[32] The struggle of families to find a suitable childcare situation is

> "Imagine if all the childcare centers closed for a week. Everything would come to a screeching halt. But you don't hear people talking about us as if we're critical to the functioning of society."[32]
> – Donna Denette, executive director of Children First

one of the main barriers to balancing the demands of work and family. With this challenge and others, women and men are constantly engaged in a never-ending dance to strike this balance, often feeling that something is getting neglected.

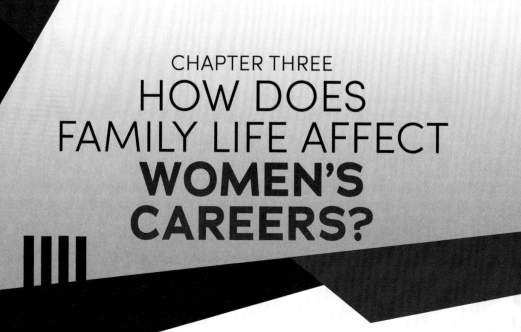

CHAPTER THREE
HOW DOES FAMILY LIFE AFFECT WOMEN'S CAREERS?

For Anne-Marie Slaughter, a former professor of politics and international affairs at Princeton University, the question of how women can achieve satisfactory work-life balance was a frustrating one. Her own experience with juggling her career and family led her to write an article in 2012 for *The Atlantic* magazine titled, "Why Women Still Can't Have It All." But what does it mean to "have it all?" In Slaughter's case, she was discussing the difficulties of trying to excel in a demanding career while also raising children in a satisfying home life. The tone of her article was somewhat rueful, as she had long believed that she had succeeded in attaining a high-powered career and content family life. Slaughter wrote:

> *I'd been the woman smiling the faintly superior smile while another woman told me she had decided to take some time out or pursue a less competitive career track so that she could spend more time with her family. I'd been the woman congratulating herself on her unswerving commitment to the feminist cause. . . . I'd been the one*

Many working women struggle to balance their jobs with taking care of their children. Society often projects an expectation onto women that they must "have it all," meaning they must be perfect mothers with highly successful careers.

telling young women at my lectures that you can have it all and do it, regardless of what field you are in.[33]

Slaughter made it clear she was writing about highly educated and ambitious women who were striving to succeed in the top levels of their fields—a rather narrow group of women. But the issue of work-life balance is a universal one, confronting all families regardless of socioeconomic status, and the options available to women vary greatly among income levels. For the one in three adult women in America on the brink of poverty, the question is not one of "having it all." These women are doing it all: working, providing for their families, taking care of their children and others, but still struggling to make ends meet.

A 2015 Pew Research Center study found that 56 percent of working parents find balancing their careers and parenting at the same time to be difficult, with 41 percent of working mothers saying that they believe being a parent has made it hard to advance professionally. There are many factors contributing to the challenges of work-life balance, and each family's situation is different. But some overarching issues that contribute to this problem include high expectations for working mothers and a lack of workplace policies to help working parents.

IMPOSSIBLE EXPECTATIONS

In the 1980s, a TV commercial advertising the perfume brand Enjoli opened with an attractive woman in a business suit singing, "I can bring home the bacon," while triumphantly fanning out a handful of money. Then she transformed to a robe-wearing housewife holding a frying pan, playfully singing, "Fry it up in a pan." But the kicker was the ending, as the woman next appears in a slinky slip of a dress while singing, "And never ever let you forget you're a man. 'Cause I'm a wooo-man."[34] The message, of course, was that a woman could work at a high-powered job while also being a supermom and attractive wife, all at the same time. While one perfume commercial can hardly be blamed for society's unrealistic stereotypes of women, it is symbolic of the message that women were receiving at the time. This message was that a woman should be able to balance her life, her job, and her children with ease.

Debora L. Spar, author of *Wonder Women: Sex, Power, and the Quest for Perfection*, discusses how the women's rights movement, particularly during the 1960s and 1970s, succeeded in opening doors that had previously been closed to women. She also writes about the unintended ways it promoted an unrealistic vision for women of the next generation: "It gave us open doors and equal opportunity, a chance to run as fast as the wind and choose the lives we wanted. And yet . . . Somehow, without meaning to—we became convinced, and then convinced [our daughters],

44

that having it all meant doing it all."[35]

The famous women who are often held up by society as role models for managing their careers and families can be both inspiring and discouraging to everyday women. Some prominent examples of this include Sheryl Sandberg, COO of Facebook and mother of two children; Marissa Mayer, who was CEO at Yahoo! and has three children; Beyoncé, singer, songwriter, businesswoman, and mother to three; and former First Lady Michelle Obama, mother to two children. These women have reached the upper levels of career success by any measure, for both women and men. They are admired and applauded for their achievements and commitment to their families. They are spokeswomen and champions for the rights of women and girls. But if women are made to believe these women represent the standard for success, then those who don't have, or don't strive for, a superstar career can easily feel like they have somehow fallen short. Instead, women need to feel supported no matter what their ambitions are. As Judith Warner described in her book *Perfect Madness: Motherhood in the Age of Anxiety*, most women and men are seeking the ability to "work a sufficient number of hours, at work they find interesting, meaningful, or enjoyable to earn enough money to buy their families a sufficiently good standard of living."[36]

> "It gave us open doors and equal opportunity, a chance to run as fast as the wind and choose the lives we wanted. And yet . . . Somehow, without meaning to—we became convinced, and then convinced [our daughters], that having it all meant doing it all."[35]
> – *Debora L. Spar, author of* Wonder Women: Sex, Power, and the Quest for Perfection

THE DUAL-CAREER JUGGLING ACT

Women and men are participating in equal numbers in the workforce, but they are still not always viewed as equals. Men are still viewed as being more responsible for financially supporting the family. This traditional view holds true even as more women are earning as much as or more than their partners. In 1980, only 13 percent of married women earned incomes that matched or exceeded their husbands' incomes. By 2000, the figure had risen to 25 percent. By 2017, 31 percent of women were earning as much as or more than their husbands or partners.

When both parents work full time, just over half (about six out of ten parents) report feeling they are doing an equal share of household tasks such as chores, disciplining children, and spending time with the kids. There are other activities, however, that appear to fall more on moms. About 54 percent of full-time working parents say the mother takes care of the children's schedules and activities. When the kids fall ill, 47 percent of moms say they are always the ones who step in to help. When couples are asked about the division of labor, more fathers than mothers see themselves as sharing the load equally. Fifty-six percent of fathers say they are doing an equal share, while only 46 percent of women agree. However, same-sex couples tend to divide tasks more equally. A 2015 survey by the Families and Work Institute found that in same-sex couples, 74 percent reported sharing routine childcare responsibilities, and 62 percent shared the tasks of caring for the kids when they were sick.

So, why don't more couples manage to create equal partnerships? Sociologist Sarah Thébaud explained, "Most people want to have more egalitarian relationships. But they may fall back on more traditional gender roles when they realize that egalitarianism is hard to achieve in the current workplace environment."[37] In other words, if workplaces offered better policies to support working families with children, more couples would be able to adopt a more equal partnership at home.

Balancing work and family is leaving dual-career parents stressed, tired, rushed, and feeling short on time to spend with their children, friends, partners, or hobbies. "You basically just always feel like you're

Research shows that mothers will step in to help more often than fathers when their children are sick. This may include taking time off of work to care for the child.

doing a horrible job at everything," said Aimee Barnes, who, along with her husband, works full time for the California Environmental Protection Agency.[38] They are parents to a fifteen-month-old son. "You're not spending as much time with your baby as you want, you're not doing the job you want to be doing at work, you're not seeing your friends hardly ever," Barnes said.[39]

> "You basically just always feel like you're doing a horrible job at everything. You're not spending as much time with your baby as you want, you're not doing the job you want to be doing at work, you're not seeing your friends hardly ever."[38]
> – Aimee Barnes, mother of a fifteen-month-old son

A typical weekday for these parents starts with an early morning getting the kids fed and ready for school or daycare, dropping them off, and then heading off to work. Once the school day is over, it often means shuttling the children to after-school care or activities, followed by arriving home for dinner, homework, and bedtime. Parents often find themselves working into the late evening to prepare for the next day.

WOMEN WORKING FROM HOME

One strategy that more women are using to manage the challenge of work-life balance is working from home. These work-at-home moms are taking advantage of modern technology to build businesses, set their own schedules, and keep their work skills up to date. By working from home, mothers are able to be more available to attend school events, manage family schedules, make dinner, and spend time with their children. But it also comes with some unique challenges. Some women working from home are working remotely for a company. They may be doing so full time, or they may be splitting time between working at home and the office. Others are working for their own business from home, while some work as freelancers or contractors. Women working for themselves can set their own schedules and choose how much to work. Tonya Abari, who runs her own business from home, only takes on jobs that work with her family schedule. "I have narrowed down a list of clients that are family-friendly and don't have unrealistic deadlines," she said.[40]

For women working remotely for a company, it can feel easy to be overlooked or forgotten by their coworkers and supervisors. Working at home can also be isolating and lonely. It requires strict discipline to stay on task when distractions lurk all around: the internet, the refrigerator, or the pile of laundry waiting to be folded. On the other hand, it is also possible to work too much. It can sometimes be hard to disconnect from work when there is no set schedule forcing an end to the work day.

LEAVING THE WORKFORCE

In 2003, the *New York Times Magazine* published an article by Lisa Belkin titled "The Opt-Out Revolution." In it, Belkin described how a group of highly educated women had left their ambitious careers because they preferred to stay at home with their children. In other words, they were "opting out." One example was Katherine Brokaw, a former lawyer. "I don't want to be on the fast track leading to a partnership at a prestigious law firm. Some people define that as success. I don't," Brokaw said.[41]

The public's response to the article was fierce, angry, and controversial. Many felt that Belkin was doing a disservice to the work of feminists from decades earlier who had fought to open the doors of opportunity to working women. Others criticized the fact that the article only focused on women who were highly educated and financially stable, as they had the option of leaving the workforce. This option is not necessarily available to middle- and lower-class women, women who are the main breadwinners for their families, or single women with no other source of income. Another strong criticism was that Belkin made it appear as though the women in her article preferred walking away from their jobs, rather than feeling they could no longer stay because their employers were inflexible regarding family needs. Belkin later agreed, writing in 2013, "I confused being pulled toward home with being pushed away from work."[42]

But why is it usually women who leave the workforce for their families, not men? One reason is simple economics: The father earns more money in 69 percent of two-income families. In only 28 percent of these

Some women choose to be stay-at-home moms simply because they want to spend more time with their children. But some mothers make this choice because they can't find ways to balance work and family.

households does the mother earn more, and in 3 percent of households, the mother and father make about the same amount. Additionally, women generally appear to be more inclined to focus on the family, while men remain focused on working to pay the bills. While it is not entirely clear why, factors such as deep-set patterns of gender roles, stereotypes reinforced by the media, and societal pressures may all contribute. A Pew Research Center poll found that public attitudes still support traditional gender roles. The survey found that one-half of Americans think that a child is better off with a mother at home, while only 8 percent say a child is better off with a stay-at-home father. However, regardless of this trend toward traditional gender roles, for women in low-income families, staying at home is often simply not an option. They stay in the workforce because they have to make money for their families.

BREADWINNER MOMS

Over the years, the number of mothers who provide the primary source of income for their families has increased. In 2014, a record 40 percent of households with children were headed by mothers who were either the primary or sole income source for the family. This is up from 11 percent in 1960. These so-called "breadwinner moms" fall into two categories. One group, 37 percent, are married mothers who have a higher income than their husbands. The other 63 percent are single moms.

Women of color are the vast majority of sole-breadwinner mothers. Seventy-one percent of African American mothers and 40.5 percent of Latina mothers are responsible for most of a family's income, compared with only 24.7 percent of white mothers.

THE NEED FOR FAMILY-FRIENDLY WORKPLACE POLICIES

Much of the challenge that parents face in their quest for better work-life balance has to do with the incompatibility of workplace policies and parents working full time. Joan Williams, author of *Unbending Gender*, described the problem: "We have a public policy that's perfectly designed for the workforce of 1960. We should have a policy designed for a workforce where 70 percent of families with children have all the adults in the labor force. That means shifting the workplace ideals from old-fashioned ideal worker to the new balanced worker, who has to balance work and family obligations."[43]

For example, the United States remains the only developed country that does not require paid maternity leave. This means new mothers often

THE STAY-AT-HOME FATHER

David Heitler-Klevans, a Pennsylvania father of two, doesn't think he deserves much praise for being a stay-at-home dad. "I thought about how women do this all the time, and it's extremely rare for anyone to . . . pat them on the back for it," he said.[1]

The number of men staying home with their kids full time has been rising. The Pew Research Center reported in 2013 that about 7 percent of fathers with children younger than age eighteen did not work outside the home, up from 4 percent in 1989.

Much of the stay-at-home parent experience is the same for women and men. Ben Sanders, father of two in Virginia, described a typical day: "You're on your feet constantly, you know—shopping, laundry, errands [and] running kids here and there." But for dads, one of the biggest challenges is making social connections. Sanders tried joining a moms' group in his neighborhood, "but didn't feel completely welcome."[2]

One of the biggest pet peeves of these fathers? "Don't call us Mr. Mom," said Chris Bernholdt, father of three in Pennsylvania. "It's like calling a working mother Mrs. Dad because she goes to an office every day."[3]

1. Quoted in Noelia Trujillo, "11 Things Stay-at-Home Dads Wish You'd Understand," Woman's Day, June 2, 2015. www.womansday.com.
2. Quoted in Jason Beaubien, "Stay-At-Home Dads Still Struggle With Diapers, Drool, Stigma and Isolation," National Public Radio, June 17, 2018. www.npr.org.
3. Quoted in Trujillo, "11 Things Stay-at-Home Dads Wish You'd Understand."

struggle deciding how much time they can spend with their newborn babies before returning to work. The US Family and Medical Leave Act (FMLA) does require up to twelve weeks of unpaid maternity leave, but it only applies to companies with fifty or more employees. Additionally, workers must have worked for the company at least one year and 1,250 hours during that year to be eligible.

Another barrier to work-life balance involves childcare. Many workplaces do not consider the difficulties parents face in matching the availability of childcare with their work schedules. For example, when in-person meetings are scheduled early in the morning or late in the afternoon, they can conflict with pick-up and drop-off times at school or childcare facilities. Additionally, when work hours fluctuate in an unpredictable way, it can be very hard to set up childcare. For example, people who work part time, such as in food service, may work seven hours one week and thirty-two the next. This is especially hard for single parents, who often do not have access to backup childcare.

As long as work schedules clash with family schedules, work-life balance is nearly impossible to achieve with two parents working full time. In some jobs, the pressure to work beyond a regular eight-hour day is intense. The Center for American Progress reported that the share of all professionals working more than fifty hours a week (ten more than a standard work week) has increased since the late 1970s. Giving mothers the flexibility to determine where and when to complete their job responsibilities could help them achieve work-life balance. A flexible work schedule could include working fewer hours, compressing work hours into fewer days, or working from home.

It is abundantly clear that the structure of the family has permanently changed from the 1950s and 1960s, but public policy, workplace expectations, and societal views have been slow to change with it. "This is not an individual problem, it is a social problem," says Mary Blair-Loy, founding director of the Center for Research on Gender in the Professions at the University of California, San Diego. "This is creating a stress for working parents that is affecting life at home and for children, and we need a societal-wide response."[44]

> "This is not an individual problem, it is a social problem. This is creating a stress for working parents that is affecting life at home and for children, and we need a societal-wide response."[44]
>
> – Mary Blair-Loy, sociologist at the University of California, San Diego

WHAT IS THE FUTURE OF WOMEN AND THE FAMILY?

With marriage on a steady decline, single parenting on the rise, society judging mothers, and women struggling to achieve a satisfying work-life balance, it can be hard for mothers to not feel discouraged. But despite these challenges, there are reasons to be optimistic. The ability to legally marry is no longer restricted by race or sexual orientation. Some new family structures are improving childcare options for families. And with women making up approximately half of the nation's workforce, companies and policymakers are recognizing the need to find ways to address the disconnect between work and family priorities. The future of the family will be shaped by these changes and others amid the cultural, political, and economic landscape. As society continues to evolve and change, so will the shape and structure of the family.

DOES MARRIAGE NEED TO BE SAVED?

The steady decline in marriage in the United States has long been a cause for concern among lawmakers. Many have called for efforts to reverse the trend. Some see the drop as a sign of decline in traditional

Children who live with married parents tend to fare better in school and are less likely to be involved with crime or other destructive behaviors, research shows. However, some experts say it's much more important for a child's parents to be financially stable than to be married.

moral values. But most of the arguments in favor of boosting marriage rates focus on the benefits that marriage has on children. Two-parent households are less likely to raise children in poverty. Children growing up with married parents also tend to perform better in school and are less likely to be involved in crime or other destructive behaviors. In 2014, US Senator Marco Rubio, a Republican from Florida, called for more efforts to increase marriage as a way to combat poverty. "The greatest tool to lift children and families from poverty is one that decreases the probability of poverty by 82 percent. . . . It's called marriage," Rubio said.[45]

Others argue that encouraging low-income parents to marry and stay married is the wrong solution. An analysis done by the Council on Contemporary Families found that stronger financial security had a better impact on children than living in a family with two married parents. This suggests that rather than marriage being the key to reducing poverty, better financial stability helps strengthen marriages. In other words, poverty itself makes it hard to have a lasting and successful marriage, and financial stress on a couple's marriage can affect their children.

This may also be why there is a growing marriage gap in America. Marriage is occurring more among those in higher income brackets, in contrast to a decline among low-income people. Women with college degrees are now much more likely to be married in their early forties than those who did not finish high school. In 1990, 63 percent of those with a high school degree or less education were married. In 2015, the percentage had dropped to 50 percent, whereas 65 percent of those age twenty-five and older with a college degree were married.

Some researchers, such as sociologist Philip Cohen and historian Stephanie Coontz, suggest that there should be less focus on encouraging couples to get married. Instead, attention may be better spent on improving access to education and financial stability for those in lower income brackets. The outcome could also lead to higher rates of marriage in the future.

BEYOND THE NUCLEAR FAMILY

As the public turns away from marriage, people are also accepting different views about what it means to be a family. Marriage is no longer seen as the only way to create a family. People are seeking new ways to find companionship and support outside the traditional nuclear family. They are interested in creative living arrangements different from the typical family model. Bella DePaulo, a social scientist at the University of California, Santa Barbara, has studied the topic in depth. Her book, *How*

An increasing number of families in the United States have multigenerational homes. In these families, children, parents, and grandparents may all live together in the same house.

We Live Now, explores alternative living styles people have been exploring and adopting. Some examples of these living arrangements include cohousing communities, single mothers combining households, and multigenerational homes.

Most cohousing communities are made up of a group of private and individual homes that are located around a common area. People who choose to live in these arrangements are seeking a place where they can live independently within a close-knit social structure. Residents may be couples living with children, single parents, older couples, or single people of all ages. The community can consist of anywhere from about ten to sixty homes. The intention is to encourage interaction and connection between residents while also allowing for privacy. There are shared spaces and shared meals for whoever wants to participate.

One resident of a cohousing community in Oakland, California, explained that what she enjoyed about the arrangement was "the shared caring for the neighborhood and each other."[46] Living in a cohousing community allows residents to share the work and expense of maintaining common areas. They help one another with meals, yard work, repairs, and childcare. By combining their talents and resources, residents can help reduce expenses, avoid social isolation, and create a ready support group for one another.

SINGLE MOTHERS BANDING TOGETHER

Carmel Sullivan's seventeen-year marriage ended in 1999, and she and her seven-year-old son, Cooper, were on their own. When the crushing loneliness left her crying herself to sleep at night, she knew something had to change. One day, inspiration hit, and she found a house big enough for more than just herself and Cooper. Then she placed an ad with a local rental service for another single mom to share their space. Sullivan was surprised when her ad received responses from eighteen other single moms. After another month, she invited one mother and her two sons to live in their home with her and Cooper.

This experience led Sullivan to develop a website to help other single mothers find similar arrangements. In 2000, she founded CoAbode, an online matching service for single mothers interested in sharing a home with other single mothers. The idea took off, and by 2018, more than 100,000 single moms across the United States had profiles on the site. The concept has been working so well, Sullivan has plans to expand the site and also include a matching program for single dads in the future.

Sharing a home with another single mother helps these women lower their living expenses, share resources, and help one another with childcare. It also provides companionship for the mothers and their children. Sullivan goes so far as to say sharing tasks with another mother is better than with a husband. As a single mother living alone, "you're the chauffeur, and doing the laundry and the homework, and there's shopping, and then all of that and the house cleaning. That all gets cut in half when you have another single mother there. That does not happen when you have a husband," she said.[47]

> "You're the chauffeur, and doing the laundry and the homework, and there's shopping, and then all of that and the house cleaning. That all gets cut in half when you have another single mother there. That does not happen when you have a husband."[47]
> – Carmel Sullivan, single mom and founder of CoAbode, an online housing service for single moms

MULTIGENERATIONAL HOMES

Studies consistently show that children raised by married parents tend to be more successful in school and less likely to engage in risky behaviors than children raised in other family situations, such as cohabitating or single-parent households. Social scientist DePaulo was interested in how children raised in multigenerational homes fared. A multigenerational home has two or more adult generations, such as a parent with children and their grandparents, all in the same home. DePaulo found that when children of divorced or never-married single parents were raised in multigenerational homes, they did just as well as those raised by married parents. They were no more likely to smoke, drink, or engage in sex at an early age, and they were just as likely to graduate from high school and go to college.

DePaulo's findings indicate that single parents can provide a more financially stable and nurturing environment for their children by choosing to live in a multigenerational home. The arrangement requires mutual respect and clear boundaries from all participants. Brianna Lewis, a single mother raising her daughter in a home with her mother and grandmother, sums up what to expect from such households: "Anyone who thinks about doing this needs to realize that there are going to be . . . challenges. It's not going to be this perfect world. . . . It takes effort [from everyone involved] to make it work."[48]

> "Anyone who thinks about doing this needs to realize that there are going to be . . . challenges. It's not going to be this perfect world. . . . It takes effort [from everyone involved] to make it work."[48]
> – Brianna Lewis, single mother living in a multigenerational household

Multigenerational family living decreased in the United States from 21 percent in 1950 to only 12 percent in 1980. But the trend started increasing in the 1980s and has continued to grow. In 2000, 15 percent of the population lived in multigenerational households. By 2016, the rate had reached 20 percent of the population. Asian and Hispanic households are driving the upward trend, as these groups are more likely than white people to live with multiple generations of a family under the same roof.

MOTHERHOOD PENALTY VS. FATHERHOOD BONUS

Research has shown that mothers face disadvantages in the workplace compared with their coworkers who do not have children. This treatment is referred to as a motherhood bias or motherhood penalty. Employers have been shown to be less likely to hire or promote a woman and more likely to pay her a lower salary if she is a mother.

Fathers, on the other hand, actually experience the opposite, often called a fatherhood bonus. Employers see men as more committed to their jobs when they have a child to support. Men's incomes go up an average of 6 percent when they have children. However, when men take parental leave or ask for any family-friendly accommodations, they are likely to lose the fatherhood bonus. More than that, these fathers are more likely than other male workers to be teased, bullied, or discriminated against at work. They also face a greater chance of being demoted or downsized and make significantly less money over the long run. These factors discourage fathers from taking paternity leave.

These biases are notoriously difficult to pinpoint and overcome. Often, people are not even aware they are treating mothers and fathers differently. So, what can be done? Shelley J. Correll, a sociologist who has conducted research on the motherhood penalty, offers some hope. Correll suggests that policies that address the deep, cultural aspects of biases against mothers can help change those biases. Companies need to redefine what it means to be a good and productive worker to reduce expectations that workers will sacrifice their family lives to be considered productive. Companies also need to adopt policies that recognize all workers have needs outside of work and recognize that productive work can be done outside of the physical workplace.

FAMILY-FRIENDLY WORK PROGRAMS

While changes in government policies and cultural biases are slow to develop, there are many companies taking the lead toward accommodating working parents. These businesses realize that it makes sense to take steps to help employees achieve work-family balance. Employers want to keep talented workers, and employees who feel their companies are accommodating to their family lives may be less likely to leave their jobs.

For thirty-two years, *Working Mother* magazine has compiled a list of the 100 best companies for working women. Companies that offer fully paid maternity leave, flexible work schedules, and childcare support are usually on the list. More companies are also providing support for the care of elderly family members, professional development for women, and help to new mothers transitioning back into work.

Of the companies on the list that provide childcare support, some include on-site childcare facilities. Patagonia, a clothing company, has a childcare center located at the company's headquarters in California. The company even provides buses to pick up and deliver kids from local schools for an after-school program. Internet company Google has four childcare centers near its campus in Mountain View, California. Goldman Sachs, an investment services company in New York, offers backup childcare to employees either at home or at the office.

Some companies have programs to support employees' older kids as well. Software company SAS offers a scholarship program for kids getting ready to enter college. For younger kids, the company has an on-site summer camp at its North Carolina headquarters.

Adobe Systems, a computer software company, provides access to college coaches to help high school kids with college strategies and advise them on schools that match their interests. "It saves me thousands of dollars," said Barbara Dieker, a single mom to two teenagers and Adobe's senior director of customer research and insights. "I make a great living at Adobe, but this is money that I don't have to apply to making college trips. I can use it elsewhere."[49]

Many of the companies on the *Working Mother* list offer other programs that go beyond paid leave and childcare. Kim Skinner works from home for Monsanto in Illinois. When she took a trip to the agriculture company's St. Louis, Missouri, headquarters, she wanted to bring her baby along. Monsanto paid for Skinner's mom to join them so she could take care of the baby while Skinner was working.

Several companies offer family-friendly programs for their employees. This may include allowing parents to work at home when needed, paid maternity leave, or after-school programs for employees' children.

Some companies go even further to help working mothers. Social media company Facebook provides a $20,000 benefit to cover fertility treatments, which help women who are having difficulties becoming pregnant. Accounting firm Ernst & Young offers free hospital-grade breast pumps and access to lactation consultants to help women with breastfeeding problems. Telecommunications company Vodafone provides employees with a thirty-hour work week at full-time pay for their first six months after parental leave. A list of company benefits such as these would not have existed fifty years ago. As more companies strive to help working mothers (or mothers-to-be) manage the challenges of parenthood, they also help to make such policies become more widespread.

WHAT GOVERNMENT POLICIES ARE NEEDED?

There are many changes to government policy that experts say could help working mothers. One important change would be for the government to offer more financial assistance for childcare. There are already some government programs that offer this, but there is not enough funding to provide financial assistance to all families in need. With the average cost of full-time childcare at close to $1,000 a month, many American families are spending more on childcare than on food and rent. Providing more childcare subsidies to help parents afford these costs would make childcare more accessible, especially for low-income families.

Another policy change that could help families would be a federal requirement for paid family leave. According to the US Bureau of Labor Statistics, only 13 percent of workers have access to paid family leave from their employers. While FMLA does provide twelve weeks of unpaid leave, many companies are exempt from this requirement. As much as 40 percent of the workforce is not covered by FMLA. Additionally, even when employees do qualify for the unpaid leave, many families can't afford to have one parent go twelve weeks without pay. Giving employees the benefit of paid family leave has been shown to improve employee health, lead to better employee retention, and boost a company's brand and reputation.

HOW WILL WOMEN BALANCE WORK AND FAMILY?

The women's rights movement of the last fifty years succeeded in creating a whole world of opportunities available to women that did not exist before. But despite the progress that has been made, changes are still needed for there to be a better balance between work and family. *New York Times* columnist Gail Collins explains: "The feminist movement of the late twentieth century created a new United States in which women ran for president, fought for their country, argued before the Supreme Court, performed heart surgery, directed movies, and flew into space. But it did not resolve the tensions of trying to raise children and hold down a job at the same time."[50]

> "The feminist movement of the late twentieth century created a new United States in which women ran for president, fought for their country, argued before the Supreme Court, performed heart surgery, directed movies, and flew into space. But it did not resolve the tensions of trying to raise children and hold down a job at the same time."[50]
> – Gail Collins, *New York Times columnist*

Researchers and business leaders who have studied and written about professional women offer some different suggestions for what women should do to attain work-family balance. For example, Sheryl Sandberg, COO of Facebook, urges women to strive for the highest goals they can in their careers. "Lean in," she told a graduating class of women at Barnard College in 2011. "Put your foot on the gas pedal and leave it there."[51] Sandberg's message was that by reaching their full potential professionally, these young women would have better options available to them if they were ever faced with making a choice between their career or their family.

Still, many young women (particularly millennials, those born roughly between 1980 and 2000) see leaving the workforce to focus on their children as a real possibility. A 2013 study by *Working Mother* magazine found 60 percent of millennials believe one parent should stay home with the children. This is an increase of 10 percent over the previous generation. A 2016 study by the ManpowerGroup, a staffing and job recruitment company, showed 61 percent of millennial women anticipated taking a break in their careers after having children.

On the other hand, Anne-Marie Slaughter, CEO of New America, a Washington, DC, think tank, suggests taking a middle path. She proposes women follow a career path with some periods of intensity and some periods of stepping back. If given the choice, Slaughter urges women not to drop out of their career paths, but to defer moving forward in their careers if needed. In other words, take a break from a career, but not a permanent one. "Plan for leaning back as well as leaning in," she says.[52] Lisen Stromberg, an advertising executive and author of the book *Work Pause Thrive*, agrees. Stromberg calls it pausing rather than leaning back, but the approach is the same: temporarily adjusting one's priorities to focus on personal goals, such as raising children, over a career. The pause can take different forms: downshifting to part-time or flexible work or temporarily leaving the workforce. In her book, Stromberg summarizes the outcome of the pausing strategy by quoting one woman who had done so herself: "I discovered I could have it all, just not all at once."[53]

> "I discovered I could have it all, just not all at once."[53]
>
> – *A working mother*

THE CHANGING FAMILY PORTRAIT

Moving toward the future, women will continue adjusting to the changing structure of the family. It is clear that women and mothers are in the workforce to stay, and women are contributing to the family income as much as or more than their partners. As a result, women have pushed for changes in the role they play within the family, resulting in women and men moving toward a more equal partnership in meeting the needs of their families. While research shows that women continue to do more household tasks than their partners, this workload has increasingly become more evenly split. Within same-sex households, the division of labor tends to be balanced.

THE COST OF RAISING A CHILD

Having a baby requires a great deal of preparation. This includes having prenatal health exams, taking pregnancy and parenting classes, and getting the home ready for a new member of the family. But perhaps one of the most important steps is one that is sometimes overlooked: Starting to save money.

According to a report released by the US Department of Agriculture in 2017, the estimated cost of raising a child from birth to age seventeen is $233,610 for a middle-class family with married parents. That doesn't include the cost of sending a child to college.

From birth to age seventeen, housing is the biggest expense, taking up 29 percent of the cost. Next comes food, at 18 percent, followed by childcare and education, at 16 percent. Other major costs include transportation, health care, and clothing.

While one might think the seemingly never-ending need for diapers and other baby-related items would make infancy the most expensive stage of childhood, kids actually become more expensive as they get older. Between birth and age two, a child costs parents about $12,680 a year. By the time they reach age fifteen, the annual cost is about $13,900.

Still, parents say children are worth the financial cost. In *Parents* magazine, New York mother Kathy Radigan says, "Having my children was such a life-altering experience. I always was looking for the purpose in my life and when I had my children I found it. . . . I wouldn't trade my best day before kids for my worst day with kids!"

Quoted in Ashley Werner, "The Real Joys of Being a Mom," Parents, n.d.
www.parents.com.

Another trend likely to continue is the rise in single-parent households, most of which are led by mothers. One twist to this trend is the increase in the number of single mothers by choice. While births to unwed teen mothers fell between 2002 and 2012, more older single women are having children. There are even support groups, such as the online group Single Mothers By Choice, to offer advice, support, and community to these women.

Families are also likely to continue becoming more racially and culturally diverse. Interracial marriage will likely continue on its upward

The family structure will continue to change, getting further and further away from the stereotypical 1950s nuclear family. Mothers will continue to adapt to their changing roles in the family.

trend. The United States is seeing increased racial and cultural diversity, a trend that will likely be reflected in marriages. Increased diversity in marriages will also be driven by the fact that US-born children and grandchildren of immigrants are more likely to marry outside of their race.

Another trend that is expected to continue is the rise in same-sex marriages. Since same-sex marriage became legal nationwide in 2015, marriages among LGBTQ (lesbian, gay, bisexual, transgender, and queer) adults has increased. According to a Gallup survey, 61 percent of cohabitating same-sex couples have married since the court ruling, up from 38 percent prior to the ruling.

WHAT DOES THE FUTURE LOOK LIKE?

As families of the modern era reflect many of the societal changes that have taken place over time, women, in their essential role within the family institution, have the ability to significantly influence how the family structure will continue to evolve in the future. Still, some worrisome trends show signs of persisting. Too many single mothers continue to live in poverty. Wages for women of color, especially African American women and Hispanic women, have remained low. Families are likely to continue to struggle to manage the high cost of childcare.

The hope is that mothers can continue to play important roles at home, in the workplace, and in the government, and that women will also increase their influence in these areas. Many women are demanding more equal support from their partners at home in terms of childcare and maintaining a household, and the disparity between men and women in this regard has narrowed. Women are pushing for more family-friendly policies in the workplace, such as paid leave, flexible schedules, and childcare support, as evidenced by more companies offering these benefits to workers. Women are seeking more influence in government, as a record number of women chose to run for political office in 2018.

Perhaps mothers with superpowers, such as Elastigirl from *The Incredibles*, may not be part of the future. But with creative thinking and persistent effort women will continue to strive to create a world where a satisfying quality of life is available to families of all backgrounds and from all walks of life.

SOURCE NOTES

INTRODUCTION: THE EVOLUTION OF WOMEN AND THE FAMILY

1. Quoted in "'The Incredibles 2' A Modern Movie," *AMC Scene*, April 23, 2018. www.amctheatres.com.

2. Quoted in "'The Incredibles 2' A Modern Movie."

3. Gail Collins, *When Everything Changed: The Amazing Journey of American Women from 1960 to the Present*. New York: Little, Brown and Co, 2009, p. 7.

4. Debora L. Spar, *Wonder Women: Sex, Power, and the Quest for Perfection*. New York: Sarah Crichton Books, 2013, p. 7.

5. Natalie Angier, "The Changing American Family," *New York Times*, November 25, 2013. www.nytimes.com.

CHAPTER 1: WHAT IS THE HISTORY BEHIND WOMEN AND THE FAMILY?

6. Stephanie Coontz, *Marriage, a History*. New York: Viking, 2005, p. 4.

7. Marilyn Yalom, *A History of the Wife*. New York: HarperCollins, 2001, p. 70.

8. Coontz, *Marriage, a History*, p. 8.

9. Quoted in Alice Kessler-Harris, *Out to Work: A History of Wage-Earning Women in the United States*. New York: Oxford University Press, 2003, p. 296.

10. Quoted in Coontz, *Marriage, a History*, p. 232.

11. Quoted in Stanley I. Kutler, *Dictionary of American History*. New York: Charles Scribner's Sons, 2003, p. 314.

12. Quoted in Carl N. Degler, At Odds: Women and the Family in America from the Revolution to the Present. New York: Oxford University Press, 1980, pp. 8–9.

13. Betty Friedan, *The Feminine Mystique*. New York: Norton, 1963, p. 9.

14. Quoted in Kelly Wallace, "Longing for the Carefree Parenting Style of Yesterday?" *CNN*, December 7, 2016. www.cnn.com.

15. Lisen Stromberg, *Work Pause Thrive*. Dallas, Texas: BenBella Books, Inc., 2017, p. 65.

16. Stephanie Coontz, *The Way We Really Are: Coming to Terms with America's Changing Families*. New York: BasicBooks, 1997, p. 65.

CHAPTER 2: WHAT CHALLENGES DO MODERN FAMILIES FACE?

17. Quoted in Coontz, *The Way We Really Are: Coming to Terms with America's Changing Families*, p. 3.

18. Quoted in Pamela Haag, "The Future of Marriage," *New York Post*, May 29, 2011. www.nypost.com.

19. Quoted in Claire Cain Miller, "Single Motherhood, in Decline Over All, Rises for Women 35 and Older," *New York Times*, May 8, 2015. www.nytimes.com.

20. Quoted in Miller, "Single Motherhood, in Decline Over All, Rises for Women 35 and Older."

21. Quoted in Kay Manning, "Why More Couples Over 50 Are Cohabitating, Not Marrying," *Chicago Tribune*, October 19, 2017. www.chicagotribune.com.

22. Quoted in Maanvi Singh, "Young Women and Men Seek More Equal Roles at Work and Home," *National Public Radio*, January 23, 2015. www.npr.org.

23. Quoted in Natasha Geiling, "Men and Women Think on Family Matters Equally, but Women Get More Stressed," *Smithsonian*, August 12, 2013. www.smithsonianmag.com.

24. Quoted in Tatiana Morales, "'The Mommy Myth.'" *CBS News*, February 4, 2004. www.cbsnews.com.

25. Quoted in Morales, "'The Mommy Myth.'"

26. Claire Howorth, "The Goddess Myth: Why Many New Mothers Feel Guilt and Shame," *Time*, October 19, 2017. www.time.com.

27. Quoted in Howorth, "The Goddess Myth: Why Many New Mothers Feel Guilt and Shame."

28. Quoted in Howorth, "The Goddess Myth: Why Many New Mothers Feel Guilt and Shame."

29. Quoted in Stella, "Woman Gets Fed Up with Mom-Shaming, Decides to Shut It Down with a Powerful Message," *Bored Panda*, n.d. www.boredpanda.com.

30. Quoted in Stella, "Woman Gets Fed Up with Mom-Shaming, Decides to Shut It Down with a Powerful Message."

31. Quoted in Stella, "Woman Gets Fed Up with Mom-Shaming, Decides to Shut It Down with a Powerful Message."

32. Quoted in "The Child-Care Crisis," *Parents*, December 6, 2017. www.parents.com.

CHAPTER 3: HOW DOES FAMILY LIFE AFFECT WOMEN'S CAREERS?

33. Anne-Marie Slaughter, "Why Women Still Can't Have It All," *The Atlantic*, July 2012. www.theatlantic.com.

34. Quoted in cosmic cosmo, "Enjoli Perfume 'Because I'm a Woman' Commercial," *YouTube*, November 30, 2014. www.youtube.com.

35. Spar, *Wonder Women: Sex, Power, and the Quest for Perfection*, p. 50.

36. Judith Warner, *Perfect Madness: Motherhood in the Age of Anxiety.* New York: Riverhead Books, 2005, p. 261.

37. Quoted in Singh, "Young Women and Men Seek More Equal Roles at Work and Home."

38. Claire Cain Miller, "Stressed, Tired, Rushed: A Portrait of the Modern Family," *New York Times*, November 4, 2015. www.nytimes.com.

39. Quoted in Miller, "Stressed, Tired, Rushed: A Portrait of the Modern Family."

40. Quoted in Rochaun Meadows-Fernandez, "More Moms of Color Are Working from Home. But That Doesn't Mean It's Easy," *Washington Post*, April 19, 2018. www.washingtonpost.com.

41. Quoted in Spar, *Wonder Women: Sex, Power, and the Quest for Perfection*, p. 184.

42. Lisa Belkin, "The Retro Wife Opts Out: What Has Changed, and What Still Needs To," *Huffington Post*, May 19, 2013. www.huffingtonpost.com.

43. Quoted in Madeleine Kunin, The New Feminist Agenda: Defining the Next Revolution for Women, Work, and Family. White River Junction, VT: Chelsea Green Pub., 2012, pp. 10–11.

44. Quoted in Miller, "Stressed, Tired, Rushed: A Portrait of the Modern Family."

CHAPTER 4: WHAT IS THE FUTURE OF WOMEN AND THE FAMILY?

45. Quoted in "Family Income—Not Married Parents—More Apt to Impact Kids' Well-Being," *NBC News*, February 27, 2015. www.nbcnews.com.

46. Quoted in Bella M. DePaulo, *How We Live Now: Redefining Home and Family in the 21st Century*. Hillsboro, OR: Atria Books/Beyond Words, 2015, p. 91.

47. Quoted in Bella DePaulo, "Meet the Woman Who Created a Craigslist for Single Moms," *Washington Post*, November 9, 2015. www.washingtonpost.com.

48. Quoted in DePaulo, *How We Live Now: Redefining Home and Family in the 21st Century*, p. 53.

49. Quoted in Katherine Reynolds Lewis, "The Amazing Ways the *Working Mother* 100 Best Companies Help Their Employees with Kids (Particularly Those with Special Needs)," *Working Mother*, September 26, 2017. www.workingmother.com.

50. Collins, *When Everything Changed: The Amazing Journey of American Women from 1960 to the Present*, p. 393.

51. "Transcript and Video of Speech by Sheryl Sandberg, Chief Operating Officer, Facebook," *Barnard College*, May 18, 2011. www.barnard.edu.

52. Anne-Marie Slaughter, *Unfinished Business*. New York: Random House, 2015, p. 194.

53. Quoted in Stromberg, *Work Pause Thrive*, p. 17.

FOR FURTHER **RESEARCH**

BOOKS

Philip N. Cohen, *Enduring Bonds*. Oakland, CA: University of California Press, 2018.

Stephanie Coontz, *The Way We Never Were: American Families and the Nostalgia Trap*. New York: Basic Books, 2016.

Bella M. DePaulo, *How We Live Now: Redefining Home and Family in the 21st Century*. Hillsboro, OR: Atria Books/Beyond Words, 2015.

Janet Lynne Golden, *Babies Made Us Modern: How Infants Brought America into the Twentieth Century*. New York: Cambridge University Press, 2018.

Liz O'Donnell, *Mogul, Mom & Maid: The Balancing Act of the Modern Woman*. Brookline, MA: Bibliomotion, 2014.

INTERNET SOURCES

Claire Howorth, "Motherhood Is Hard to Get Wrong. So Why Do So Many Moms Feel So Bad About Themselves?" *Time*, October 19, 2017. www.time.com.

Sharlene Johnson, "The Child-Care Crisis," *Parents*, December 6, 2017. www.parents.com.

Rose Leadem, "Is Work-Life Balance Even Possible? (Infographic)." *Entrepreneur*, February 18, 2018. www.entrepreneur.com.

Claire Cain Miller, "Stressed, Tired, Rushed: A Portrait of the Modern Family," *New York Times,* November 4, 2015. www.nytimes.com.

"Parenting in America," *Pew Research Center*, December 17, 2015. www.pewsocialtrends.org.

WEBSITES

Family, *The Atlantic*
www.theatlantic.com/family

The Atlantic magazine's Family online newsletter provides stories every week on the life of the family.

Lean In
www.leanin.org

The Lean In organization complements Facebook COO Sheryl Sandberg's well-known book *Lean In*. The organization aims to inspire and educate women to help them achieve their professional goals.

Pew Research Center's Social and Demographic Trends
www.pewsocialtrends.org

This project of the nonpartisan fact tank Pew Research Center examines behaviors and attitudes of Americans in different areas of their lives, including family issues.

Well Family, *The New York Times*
www.nytimes.com/section/well/family

The *New York Times*'s Well Family online section covers family, parenthood, childhood, health, and relationships.

Working Mother
www.workingmother.com

Working Mother magazine offers articles focused on parenting, careers, and work-family balance.

INDEX

IMAGE CREDITS

Cover: © Flamingo Images/Shutterstock Images

4: © Ivy Photos/Shutterstock Images

5 (top): © Dragon Images/Shutterstock Images

5 (bottom): © Lital Israeli/Shutterstock Images

7: © Sarunyu L/Shutterstock Images

11: © Thomas J. O'Halloran/U.S. News & World Report Magazine Photograph Collection/Library of Congress

14: © C. W. Turner/Library of Congress

16: © Stanley Kubrick/LOOK Magazine Photograph Collection/Library of Congress

19: © Everett Collection/Shutterstock Images

23: © DragonImages/iStockphoto

27: © PeopleImages/iStockphoto

29: © Red Line Editorial

33: © pixelheadphoto digitalskillet/Shutterstock Images

35: © Rawpixel/iStockphoto

40: © Monkey Business Images/Shutterstock Images

43: © jacoblund/iStockphoto

47: © Paul Bradbury/iStockphoto

50: © iofoto/Shutterstock Images

55: © Ivy Photos/Shutterstock Images

57: © wavebreakmedia/Shutterstock Images

63: © LightFieldStudios/iStockphoto

68: © Portra/iStockphoto

ABOUT THE **AUTHOR**

Carol Kim lives in Texas with her husband and two daughters, and she is very familiar with the challenges facing women and the family. She has written both fiction and nonfiction for children.